FIVE BRILLIANT WAYS TO USE
AI TO ATTRACT WOMEN

AI RIZZ

ENRIQUE VOLTAIRE

AUTHOR OF
How to Attract Women
IF YOU'RE NOT THAT ATTRACTIVE

AI Rizz: Five Brilliant Ways to Use AI to Attract Women*

Who Should Read This Book

This book is for the man who believes that he can attract beautiful women and find one to marry.

It's for the man who is willing to eat right, work out, and study for both personal and professional success.

It's for the man dedicated to being the best version of himself—a version women cannot ignore.

I recently learned that some animals find lifelong partners just like humans do.

They hook up, have children, and stay together until death.

And if finches, beavers, and termites can love too,

Then, dammit, **so can you!**

Finding love may not be easy,

But it's definitely possible.

And if you believe in that possibility,

Then this book is for you.

Dedication

To all men in the struggle.

Learn,
earn
grow.

The best revenge
is living well
and being happy.

--Enrique Voltaire

Contents

AIAIAIAIAIAIAIAIAIAIAIAIAIAIAIAIAIAIAIAIAIAIAIAIAIAIAIAIAIAIAIAIAIAIAIAIAIAIAIAIAIAIAI

The Five Brilliant Ways to Use AI to Attract Women

Introduction

I love AI.

It's like Google, but I don't have to scroll through pages to find an answer. AI does the searching for you and delivers a clear, immediate response. This is both a blessing and a curse.

The blessing is the speed—you get answers instantly. The curse is that the AI's response isn't always the best one and, about 15% of the time, it's just wrong.

For example, you ask AI: *Is it hot today?*

Regardless of the answer, "hot" is relative.

In New York City, 90°F in the summer is hot, but 80°F in the spring is also considered "hot." In the winter, 60°F might feel "hot" compared to freezing temperatures. So what is *hot*? The AI's answer could be right or wrong depending on your own perception.

As fast and knowledgeable as AI is, never forget that it's flawed. You cannot take everything it says as truth. You must think critically and do more research—read websites, read books, talk to experts. Talk to humans. Reflect. Talk to yourself.

Most importantly, live your life and learn from your experiences.

What is AI and How Can It Help?

If you don't know what AI is, go to chat.openai.com (you'll need to sign up with a Google account), type in a question, and see what happens.

ChatGPT—the most popular AI tool today—reads your question, searches a vast database of information, and generates an answer instantly.

What does ChatGPT stand for?

- **Chat** = It talks with you.

- **GPT** = Generative Pre-trained Transformer, so the program is "pre-trained" to "generate" answers that it will "transform" into writing you can understand.

It's fast, convenient, and surprisingly good at answering almost anything. But here's the thing: AI doesn't think—it predicts.

That means sometimes, it gets things wrong.

Take a simple question: *Is it hot today?*

"Hot" is relative. In New York City, 90°F in the summer is hot, but 80°F in the spring might also feel hot. In winter, 60°F might feel like summer compared to freezing temperatures. So what does *hot* mean? The AI will give you an answer, but whether it's "right" depends on how you define hot.

That's why you need to guide it.

- **Too complicated?** Tell it to explain like you're in 5th grade.

- **Want personality?** Ask for an answer in the style of a nosy Filipino auntie in Taglish or a Jamaican speaking patois.

- **Need creativity?** Get your answer as a poem, a rap, or in the voice of your favorite YouTuber.

Chat GPT will practically give you an answer to any question in any form with few reservations, and it will even follow up that answer with a question to make you think further about the issue.

It is a smart person in your smartphone—who is sometimes wrong.

This book is about using this technology to help you with dating.

Why I Prefer ChatGPT Plus

There are plenty of AI models out there—CoPilot, Gemini, DeepSeek, and more. But my go-to is ChatGPT Plus.

Yes, I willingly pay $20 a month for the Plus features. But when you compare that cost to other forms of education—college tuition, online courses, books—it's an absolute bargain.

Having paid college tuition this year, I can say with certainty that ChatGPT Plus has been more valuable to my education than my professors—no disrespect intended. Every fact-based question I needed answered during a lecture? ChatGPT Plus handled it instantly. And unlike the free version, I never get the dreaded messages:

- *"ChatGPT is at capacity right now due to high traffic."*

- *"You've used up all your free questions for the day."*

But ChatGPT Plus does more than just answer questions. It can analyze pictures, scan websites, process PDFs, and even summarize YouTube videos. This means it's not just a chatbot—it's a research assistant, a tutor, and a study guide, all in one.

Outside the classroom, ChatGPT Plus serves as an educator, mentor, motivator, and even an amateur psychologist. It doesn't always give perfect advice, but when I need insight or a second opinion, it's there. I can assess its response, refine it, and apply it as I see fit.

Compared to the free version, ChatGPT Plus operates on a larger database, delivers more precise responses, and even adapts to your tone. If you sound frustrated, it can adjust its response to be more soothing, mimicking a real human interaction.

At the time of writing, the latest feature—Deep Search—allows ChatGPT Plus to pull answers from multiple verified sources across the internet, essentially providing you with a research paper on demand.

For $20 a month, the education, insights, and immediate access to knowledge make it worth every penny.

And no, ChatGPT didn't pay me to say this—I'm just a regular person fascinated by what this technology can do.

So going forward in this book, when I say "AI," I'm referring to ChatGPT Plus. If the AI you're using can't do what I'm about to discuss, I highly recommend upgrading.

What is Rizz?

Rizz is short for charisma—the ability to exude confidence and attract others. A man with rizz knows how to draw women in effortlessly.

So how does a man develop rizz?

By cultivating the traits that make him naturally magnetic to women.
And what if he isn't born with the physical features that would make him traditionally handsome?

He builds himself into the kind of man women are drawn to.

- He works on his body until women are curious about what's underneath his clothes.

- He sharpens his communication skills so that people enjoy being around him.

- He learns how to make and manage money so he can introduce women to experiences they actually want to be part of.

This book is about developing true charisma—the kind that makes women notice, chase, and stay.

Using AI to Attract Women

You could ask AI, *"How do I attract women?"*—but the answer will likely be generic, unaware of your personal strengths, weaknesses, or the specific type of woman you're trying to attract.

There are some general principles that hold true:

- You need enough courage to initiate conversations and ask women out.

- You should have the financial ability to take a woman on enjoyable dates.

- You must be willing to make sacrifices if you want a relationship to progress.

Of course, cowardly, broke, and selfish men still manage to attract women. That doesn't mean the advice AI (or I) provide is wrong—it just means life is full of anomalies. The key is understanding that general advice isn't one-size-fits-all. AI can only give you a framework; it's up to you to apply it in a way that fits your life, personality, and goals.

And that's the real process of learning: gaining information, testing it in real life, analyzing the results, and adjusting as necessary. Only through experience will you discover what works for YOU and how YOU can attract the kind of women you want.

Timeless Dating Advice

I won't be discussing Tinder or any other dating app in this book. I hear it's pretty easy to find dates using them, but I don't know enough about those apps to either promote or criticize them.

I got married before the rise of dating apps, so I won't pretend to be an expert.

My advice on meeting women is based on traditional, real-world interactions—walking up to a girl, starting a conversation, and getting her phone number. Not her Snap, not her Insta, not her Tag—her actual phone number.

And honestly, you shouldn't have to depend on an app to meet women. In-person attraction will always matter.

Now, if you want to use dating apps, go ahead. Use ChatGPT to help you build your profile, assess your pictures, tweak your bio, and improve your messages. I'm all for using whatever tools work for dating.

But this book is about the traditional way to attract women— get in shape, make money, grow a pair, and talk to her.

If she enjoys the conversation, she'll give you her number so you can hang out.

If she just wants to give you her Tag or email, stay in touch and ask her out that way.

And if she's not interested in your fit, rich, chivalrous self— well, that's her loss.

AI

The Five Brilliant Ways to Use AI to Attract Women

AIAIAIAIAIAIAIAIAIAIAIAIAIAIAIAIAIAIAIAIAIAIAIAIAIAIAIAIAIAIAIAIAIAIAIAIAIAIA

Brilliant Way #1

Use AI to Get Smarter

Google *"How to attract women,"* and you'll get a flood of websites to sift through, each offering different advice. Read a few, and now you're stuck trying to figure out which advice actually applies to you.

Ask AI the same question, and you cut out the Google middleman—getting immediate, direct advice. Keep asking questions, and the AI's responses will become more tailored to your situation.

Don't agree with what AI tells you? Say so. AI will adjust.

Go out and implement the advice. Did it work? Did it fail miserably?

Come back to AI and explain what happened. Get more feedback. Make adjustments. Repeat.

Do not give up.

AI isn't always right—but neither are humans.

Ask AI for advice on anything, and as long as the advice is logical and reasonable, test it. See what happens when you actually apply it.

After all, action is the key to attracting women. You have to take the first step, push through setbacks, and keep improving. Or, you can sit on the sidelines, overthink everything, and stay exactly where you are.

The choice is yours.

Women Love Industrious Men

Industrious men are diligent and hardworking.

- Diligence means being conscious and intentional about what you're doing.

- Hard work means not being lazy.

World-renowned psychologist Jordan Peterson has lectured on how a man's industriousness is more attractive to women than his wealth alone. The matrix below illustrates this concept:

	Poor Man	**Rich Man**
Industrious	Surprisingly Attractive	Extremely Attractive
Lazy	Extremely Unattractive	Surprisingly Unattractive

Lazy poor men were seen as the least attractive—it's one thing to struggle financially, but it's worse to struggle and lack ambition.

Lazy rich men were only slightly better—wealth alone isn't enough to make a man attractive in the eyes of most women.

Rich industrious men were considered very attractive—women are drawn to men who work hard and have the resources to care for them.

But the most interesting result?

Poor industrious men were nearly as attractive as rich industrious men—and they were seen as far more desirable than lazy rich men.

Be Industrious

If you want to be attractive, work hard. It matters more than money alone.

Jordan Peterson himself is proof of this principle—he went from being a University of Toronto professor to a world-renowned expert on male self-improvement. He tells men to "bear their cross"— have a life mission, pursue it relentlessly, take full responsibility, embrace struggle as part of the journey, and remain resilient through it all.

At the end of the day, women aren't just looking for money—they're looking for drive, ambition, and a man with purpose.

Use AI as a Steppingstone for Deeper Learning

Learning is essential if you want to get anywhere in life.

Some people go as far as saying that if you're not learning, you're not really living.

Oprah Winfrey once shared that her grandfather asked her every day what she had learned. If she couldn't give him an answer, he'd make her read something until she could. That kind of mindset—seeking knowledge daily—is what separates those who grow from those who stay stagnant.

I knew nothing about dating through my early twenties. If I were attracted to a girl, I'd try to talk to her and hope she was attracted to me. Sometimes, I'd ask her to hang out, but most of the time, I wouldn't.

Then I read *How to Succeed with Women* by Ron Louis and David Copeland.

That book changed everything.

I learned that if I wanted to get dates, I shouldn't aim to be a woman's friend. In fact, I should stay as far away from the friend zone as possible. I learned to look presentable, speak with confidence, ask for her number, and move on immediately if rejected.

And suddenly, I started getting dates—all because I took the time to learn.

15

Over time, I compounded what I learned—from books, from experience, and from studying the psychology of attraction. The result? Two published dating books.

All because I chose to learn.

Today, your search for knowledge doesn't have to start with books. It doesn't have to start with sorting through countless Google search results.

It starts with you asking AI a single question.

Think of AI as a raindrop—the small start of a journey that can lead to something far greater. Your goal is to turn that raindrop into an ocean of swagger and confidence.

Start compounding drops of knowledge. Read articles. Read books. Most importantly, learn from experience.

Women love intelligent, industrious men.

Be one.

The Six Pillars of Getting Your Shit Together

Not all knowledge is equal. Not all skills are equal. Not all work is equal.

If you want to attract women, you need to get good at the right things. Women don't care how skilled an adult man is at basketball or video games—so unless you have an agent lined up, stop wasting time on trivial activities.

If you're not attracting many women right now, it's time to revamp yourself—or, as many would say, get your shit together.

What follows are *The Six Pillars of Getting Your Shit Together.* I firmly believe that by working on these six foundational areas, you will transform into a better, more desirable man—one worthy of any woman's attention.

I. Physical Fitness

Every man should understand which foods fuel his body and which ones work against it. You can't eat mindlessly. When you're young, you might be able to get away with eating whatever you want thanks to fast metabolism or lucky genetics. But as you age, that changes. Eventually, you'll realize that not eating well means not feeling well.

Every man should also know how to take care of his body. I learned this firsthand. I took an exercise course in college, studied fitness and nutrition on my own, and committed to a lifestyle of eating well and staying active. Did I become a bodybuilder? No. But I got in good enough shape to start attracting dates.

And that's the point. You don't have to be a bodybuilder. But if you let yourself go, attracting women will be more difficult.

If you want to succeed—not just in attracting women, but in life—you need to understand the importance of exercise and nutrition and follow the rules. Your body is the foundation for everything you do. Ignore it, and you'll struggle. Master it, and you'll have an advantage over every man who doesn't.

II.   **Emotional Intelligence**

Every man should know how to manage his emotions. You can't keep losing your cool and expect it not to affect the people around you.

If you constantly lash out and push loved ones away, it's only a matter of time before temporary negativity turns into permanent consequences.

Learn to coexist with the demon within you. Train yourself to make consistent, good decisions that lead to long-term success. Handle stress constructively—use it as fuel to become a better man instead of letting it consume you.

And if controlling your emotions feels impossible, don't rely solely on AI.

And if you struggle to control your emotions, consider working with a professional who can help.

III.   **Financial Intelligence**

You won't learn everything you need to know about money from AI—but it's a good start.

Learn how money works. Then go out and earn it. Keep learning, keep earning. That cycle should never stop. It starts with your childhood allowance and ends with your retirement account.

Read foundational advice from people like Dave Ramsey and Ramit Sethi. Studying things like 401(k)s, Roth IRAs, high-yield savings accounts, and low-cost index funds might not be as entertaining as anime or social media, but it's far more useful than most of what you'll learn in college.

Most people reading this have access to public schools, libraries, and the internet. That means the tools for understanding money—and building wealth—are already within reach.

No one's going to sit you down and teach you how to grow your money. That's your job. And you should take it seriously—because learning how to grow your money is more important than just earning it.

Use AI to kickstart your financial education. Ask smart questions. Read the answers carefully. Dig deeper. Learn from books, articles, and credible sources.

Keep learning. Keep earning. Your future self is counting on it.

And remember—making money doesn't just improve your lifestyle. It makes you more attractive. Women notice men who take care of their finances.

IV.   **Understanding Women**

Women are confusing. Let's just admit it.

Learning how to understand them is a real skill—and one you can improve with time, effort, and the right tools. Use AI. Read books. Interact with women in real life.

Navigating relationships is harder than learning how to grow money. Just look at some of the most successful men on the planet—Bill Gates, Jeff Bezos, Elon Musk. These are men who built empires and earned billions... and still faced challenges in marriage.

Finding the right woman is possible. But living "happily ever after" is harder than you've been told.

Learn how to introduce yourself with confidence.
Learn how to read a woman's tone and body language.
Learn how to ask for her number—and handle her answer, whatever it is.

Then take it further.
Learn what makes a relationship grow.
Learn what keeps a good woman happy.
Learn what it takes to stay married—and what it takes to stay sane in the process.

And even if things don't go how you planned... even if your relationship ends or your marriage doesn't last forever... don't fall apart.

Learn from the experience. Carry the wisdom forward. And always protect the three essentials: Your physical health, your mental health, and your money.

Because understanding women is powerful.

But understanding yourself is essential.

V.   **Critical Thinking**

Learn how to think for yourself.

There's no one-size-fits-all fitness plan, mental health solution, financial strategy, or perfect woman.

- The best workout and diet plan is the one you can consistently follow.

- The right mental health practice is the one that actually works.

- A smart financial plan depends on your age, your goals, and your risk tolerance.

- The best woman for you isn't the one you can live with—she's the one you can't live without.

Know what you want, go after it, and be willing to adjust.

The only consistency in life is inconsistency.

Just when you think you've got a handle on things, life will throw something at you that shakes everything up— something that forces you to be stronger, smarter, and more grounded.

Some things in this book won't work for you.
Some things will.

Analyze what's useful and what's not *for your own situation.*

VI. **Sacrifice**

A man who has it together understands sacrifice.

He sacrifices short-term pleasure to be at work, in the gym, or with his family—because he sees the big picture.

He knows what he ultimately wants, and he's working toward that goal, whether he enjoys it or not.

If you want the American Dream—marriage, kids, a house with a white picket fence—you're going to have to give up a lot.

Unless you were born into outrageous wealth, you'll need to grind. And even if you were—you'll still have to sacrifice. Often, that sacrifice is harder, because it's not about survival; it's about meaning.

Look at the lives of celebrity children—people with every advantage, and yet many of them struggle.

Sacrifice takes a toll on everyone. Don't be afraid to use the tools around you—AI, mentors, faith, therapy, brotherhood—to help you manage the weight of doing things you despise in order to live a life you love.

People have sacrificed for you, whether you realize it or not. And if you're lucky enough to live a full, fruitful life, you'll make that same sacrifice for others.

The Pillars' Order of Importance

You should have your life in order—whether you plan to attract a woman or not.

Because seriously, what is the alternative?

How you do anything is how you do everything.

If you half-ass your work, your body, your habits, your relationships—guess what? You're going to live a half-ass life.

But going 100% all day, every day? That's not the answer either. You'll burn out.

Most of us aren't mailing it in, but we're not going as hard as we could, either.

My advice: Do your best. Then do a little better tomorrow.

And if you don't know where to start?

Start with the first pillar—Physical Fitness.

Don't wait until you've "mastered" one area of life before touching the next. Just get good at one pillar, then move on to the next. And the next.

Here's a more detailed breakdown for getting your life together:

I.   Physical Fitness

Get yourself healthy—for yourself. And yes, being in shape will increase your chances of attracting a future mate.

Being physically healthy boosts your confidence, improves your posture, and sharpens your energy. Exercise releases endorphins, reduces stress, and helps regulate your mood—all of which make you a more emotionally intelligent man.

II.   Emotional Intelligence

Work on your body before you work on your mind.

Most people think they need to be motivated before they act. But the truth is, you usually have to act before you feel anything.

Don't wait until you feel like exercising —just move. Put in the reps. And once you start moving, you'll start feeling different. Emotions follow action.

Get moving, and your mood will shift. Keep moving, and your mind will catch up. That's the foundation of emotional intelligence: learning how to manage your mind by mastering your actions.

III.   Financial Intelligence

Being rich doesn't mean much if you're not physically or emotionally fit.

If you doubt that, just look at the lives of the rich and famous who broke down mentally, physically, or both.

Get your body and mind right before you get your money right.

But make no mistake—money matters. You'll need it to create the time, space, and resources to keep your body strong and your mind clear.

IV.   Understanding Women

Before you start trying to attract women, get your own life in order.
Get physically healthy.
Get emotionally healthy.
Get financially healthy.

Think of the airplane rule: put your oxygen mask on first, then help others.
The same goes here—build yourself up before bringing someone else into your world.

A beautiful woman won't give you a meaningful life; a meaningful life will attract beautiful women.

Live a strong, disciplined life first—and then you'll be ready to attract the kind of woman who belongs in it.

V.   Critical Thinking

Never stop growing.

Once you're fit, rich, and taken, keep studying success.

Learn what works for you. Learn what works for others.
Learn from experience—especially your own.

Life will test you. Persevere.

Build a treasure of a life—and protect it.

Don't let anything or anyone—especially yourself—screw it up.

VI.   Sacrifice

You need money to give money.

Similarly, you need to get your shit together before you can help other people—your wife, your kids, family and friends in need, or even charity—get their shit together.

These life skills aren't just important for attracting women; they are important building a great life. It is easy for me to tell you to get your life in order according to the six pillars. However, life isn't linear. You may be called upon to help a sick loved one when you yourself are out of shape, depressed, broke, scared, and lonely.

Make the necessary sacrifices. Do what you can. Save those you can save and, simultaneously, find a way to save yourself. Do your best to get your shit together but be aware that there will be a time when shit hits the fan. And what do you do then? The only thing you can do—your best.

Get Smarter without AI

The title of this book might suggest that AI alone can help you attract women—but that's only part of the truth.

AI is a starting point. A tool. A place to begin learning.

Because when it comes to getting better at anything—whether it's playing basketball, writing a book, or attracting women—you have to do the actual work.

Why?

Because doing the work means making mistakes.

And learning from those mistakes is how you grow.

When you were a baby, you fell learning to walk.

You stuttered learning to talk.

And you pissed yourself learning to use the toilet.

That's how humans learn—by screwing up and trying again.

So yes—use AI. Use this book. They'll help you get better.

But the work doesn't end there.

Read more books. Try more advice.

Keep what works. Throw out what doesn't.

Some believe the best way to find a girlfriend is to be a girl's friend—to go from friendzone to endzone.

I learned that the best way to get a girlfriend was to hit on a woman and quit on her if she wasn't feeling me.

So what's the right approach?

The one that works for you.

That's the paradox: there's no one-size-fits-all approach to attracting women.

There are basic skills, sure—but the details vary.

Use AI to learn the basics.

But as you grow, develop your own method.

Because at some point, you'll need to be smarter than AI.

You'll need to develop real, human intelligence—

if you want to succeed with women... and in life.

Brilliant Way #2

Use AI to Get Fit

I've exercised regularly since college. I didn't always hit the gym, but I played basketball at the park—an activity fewer young people seem to care about these days.

I took an exercise class in college, did calisthenics here and there, and even hired a personal trainer—both in person and, for two years, over Zoom[1].

I also went through a phase where I thought I could lose weight just by "eating right" and skipping workouts. That

---

[1] You can email my personal trainer at dedioscarlo1@yahoo.com if you want to know his rates.

ended in disaster. I stopped exercising… and kept eating poorly, like usual.

These days, I'm learning firsthand what it means to lose the speed of your metabolism as you age:

- In your 20s, you can eat like trash, hit the gym, and still look decent.
- In your 30s, you have to start watching what you eat—but regular exercise can still keep you in shape.
- In your 40s, you **have to** eat well *and* exercise. There's no way around it.
- I haven't hit my 50s yet, but based on everything I've read, things don't magically improve. Your metabolism slows down further, your recovery takes longer, and the consequences of laziness show up faster.

But at least I have AI now.

I can ask it anything—diet, fitness, training plans, macros, fasting, muscle groups—and get instant answers. It's like having a coach in my pocket 24/7.

Why Women Love Fit Men

Humans, like animals, are biologically wired to reproduce. It's primal—survive and pass on your genes. And who do women instinctively want to reproduce with? Healthy men—tall. Broad shoulders. Lean. Strong. Bright smile. Full head of hair.

Think Gaston from Beauty and the Beast—minus the narcissism and malice.

Does that mean short, obese, bald men are doomed to die alone? Of course not. But it does mean they'll have a harder time attracting women.

Fortunately, men have a secret weapon: status and wealth.

A man might not look like the ideal physical specimen, but if he has money and influence, women will take notice. Why? Because wealth signals stability, power, and the ability to provide—all traits tied to survival and long-term security.

But here's the thing: most young men aren't rich yet.

So if you don't have wealth, you'd better look healthy.

Get in shape. Burn fat. Build muscle. Develop strength and stamina. Send the message that your genes are worth passing on. Women absolutely look at a man's body and picture what he'd be like in bed. That's not shallow. That's biology.

Strong, fit men are attractive.

Even if you're already rich, be a strong, fit man anyway.

Because the ultimate flex is having both: Strength and status.

Use AI to Understand Basic Nutrition

Think before you put anything into your body.

Understand the basics: lean protein fills you up, vegetables with fiber help your digestion, and sugar and refined carbs make you want more sugar and carbs—a cycle that's hard to break.

The typical American diet—loaded with hamburgers, hot dogs, fries, and pizza—is unhealthy. By contrast, the Mediterranean diet, built around fish, vegetables, salad, and extra virgin olive oil, is widely considered one of the healthiest in the world.

Sure, eating out is fun—but doing it all the time usually leads to poor choices. Healthy meal planning at home isn't just better for your body—it saves money and might even save your life.

Now, if you ever have questions or you're not sure if something you're about to eat is good for you—ask AI.

I've asked AI why I crave sugar and what I can do about it. I've learned that a chicken breast salad clocks in around 390 calories and leaves me feeling full. Half an Italian BMT from Subway? 450 calories—and it just makes me want the other half.

When I get a stomach ache, I'll tell AI what I ate, and it offers possible explanations and suggestions. I've even asked if Pepto Bismol would help, and AI will break down how it works and when it's appropriate.

Has AI motivated me to eat right? Hardly.

But it has made me more aware of what's good for me and what's not. And when it comes to the middle-aged battle of the bulge, that awareness is half the fight.

Use AI as a Personal Trainer

If you know how to use AI, then you've basically got a personal trainer, coach, and mentor in your pocket.

Want to get better at basketball? Weightlifting? Running? Just ask AI:

- *How do I work on my dribbling without a basketball?*
- *Give me a plan to lift heavier after plateauing on my bench press.*
- *Create a plan for me to run a mile under 8 minutes.*

The feedback you get isn't from some random guy on the playground or that know-it-all at the gym. It's researched, clear, and tailored to how you want it—whether that's plain and simple, eighth-grade level, or narrated like a voice-over from Arnold Schwarzenegger.

No pricey trainers. No bloated coaching fees.
Just free, calculated advice—ready when you are.

A real plan, easy to tweak, right there in your hand.

You just have to ask.

Everyone Knows If You Workout

Shoutout to Evan—the brolic barista at the Starbucks drive-thru window.

You can tell he works out. His massive arm extends through every car window, handing people their drinks, making Venti cups look like Dixie cups.

The first time I saw him, I said, "Dude, your arms are massive. How often do you work out?"

Pause.

"Thanks, dude!" he replied, all cheerful and Keanu Reeves–in–Point Break. "I try to work out four to five days a week."

Then he hit me with one of the most unexpectedly philosophical statements I've ever heard about exercise:

> *You know, working out is like the only sport you can do where everyone knows you do it. Think about it—you don't know if someone plays basketball or skateboards just by looking at them. But if someone works out? You can tell.*

Boom.

Work out, and everyone will know.

Remember: Humans are wired to look for mates with strong, healthy genes to pass on. That's evolutionary biology. That's survival. And by working out, you're telling the world—especially the ladies—my genes are worth continuing.

And now that AI is a personal trainer in your pocket, you have zero excuse not to know what to do.

Tell AI your goal. Ask it to build a workout plan.
Adjust as needed.

Lift weights. Do cardio. Eat right.

And yeah—everyone will notice.

The Psychological Impact of Being Fit

I was fit once—it's a great feeling.

You fit into all your clothes. You can tuck in your shirt without sucking in your gut. You can run after a beautiful woman you want to talk to without being out of breath.

Women wonder if you've got a six-pack—and even if you don't, the mystery alone works in your favor. I was never Mr. Olympia or Brad Pitt, but I had a chest that puffed out over my gut—not the other way around.

When you're fit, you stand taller. You sit straighter. You carry yourself with the confidence of a man who knows he's a good catch in the gene pool.

Here's the thing: Women are hardwired for survival. They don't have the luxury of being careless when choosing a partner.

One-on-one, they're more vulnerable to violence—so evolution trained them to assess men quickly: for strength, safety, and the capacity to protect or destroy.

In general, women are better judges of character than men—because they have to be. Their safety, and the future of their kids, depends on it.

And obviously, being overweight or out of shape doesn't help you in that assessment.

So what do you do?

Get strong. Get fit. Walk better. Talk better.

Exude the confidence of a man who takes care of himself.

Become a paragon of health and discipline.

You don't need to look like an Olympian to attract women.

But looking like you could carry her up five flights of stairs without dying?

That wouldn't hurt.

Look your best.

Feel your best.

Be your best.

Women will notice.

And the ones who don't?

They're the ones missing out.

Brilliant
Way #3

Use AI to
Make Money

If you're broke, ask AI how to make money.
It's that simple.

You'll get suggestions—some basic, some creative—and AI
might even ask you back:

> *What do you like to do for fun?* or
> *What are you legally willing to do to make money?*

It'll break down the difference between short-term
gains and long-term wealth.
It'll teach you about calculated risk, investments, and the
difference between liabilities and assets.

And beyond wages and salaries, there are tons of ways to build wealth: 401(k), 403(b), Roth IRA, CDs, ETFs, stocks, bonds, low-cost index funds, side businesses, royalties, rentals, etc.

Life isn't fair: Some are born into wealth. Most of us aren't. Some are raised with financial literacy while most of us are taught nothing—or worse, taught wrong:

• "Pay the minimum on your credit card balance."
• "Renting a home is like throwing money away."
• "Leasing a car saves money."

Here's the good news: You can change that.

You can either complain about the system—
Or you can learn the game and play to win.

I chose to learn.
I read the books. I made investments. I gained. I lost.

But most importantly? I learned.
And now I can pass that knowledge on to my children.

What will you teach yours?

Women Love Financially Stable Men

Since the beginning of time, women have sought men who can provide.

Back in the caveman days, the man went out to hunt saber-toothed tigers while the woman tended to the cave and raised the cave couple's babies. Fast-forward 10,000 years—and despite what a few TikTok personalities may scream into their ring lights—not much has changed.

Women are still attracted to men who can provide. Only now, instead of dragging home dead animals, men bring home money—so women can go to the store, buy dead animals, and cook.

The lesson: Be the man who brings home some money.

Now, you might think I'm setting you up to attract a gold digger.

Well, some women *will* take advantage of you. That's why you need the wisdom to spot the difference between a potential wife who is a giver—and a bloodsucking leech who is a taker.

And please, don't be the guy who spends money on a woman and expects sex in return. That's not masculinity. That's immaturity.

Who you date and who you marry is always a gamble. Sometimes you invest your money and emotions—and you

45

get a beautiful return.

Other times, you go all in—and end up broke and brokenhearted.

That's life.

Don't be angry. Don't get bitter. And don't be that guy on TikTok complaining about how hard it is out there.

That helps no one.

Teach Yourself to Be Rich

After finding the love of my life as a result of reading dating books, I found myself financially desperate.

So, I went back to the same formula—educating myself out of a rut—and began reading all I could on how to make money.

If you're going to embark on that same journey to achieve riches beyond your wildest dreams, here are the top ten books I recommend—in no particular order.

1.   *Rich Dad Poor Dad* by Robert Kiyosaki

Buy assets—things that bring in money—as opposed to liabilities—things that force you to spend more money. Kiyosaki explains the difference between working for money and having money work for you.

2.   *The Millionaire Next Door* by Thomas J. Stanley and William D. Danko

Most millionaires have stable jobs, great retirement packages, and live in middle-class neighborhoods. They drive reliable used cars instead of flashy, expensive ones. Stanley and Danko show that wealth is about discipline, not appearances.

3. *Secrets of the Millionaire Mind* by T. Harv Eker

Most of us have learned how to use money incorrectly.
Eker teaches people to rethink conventional thoughts about
wealth. For example: *Rich people admire other rich and successful
people. Poor people resent them.* Mind blown yet?

4. *I Will Teach You to Be Rich* by Ramit Sethi

Budget by spending money on what you love and cutting
mercilessly on everything else. Sethi tells you to automate
your finances and put your savings into investments like
VTSAX, a low-cost index fund. Practical, no-nonsense advice
on how to build real wealth.

5. *Think and Grow Rich* by Napoleon Hill

Know exactly what you want and what you're willing to do to
achieve it. Then take consistent action to make it happen. Hill
emphasizes that success starts with clear intent and
unwavering persistence.

6. *The Personal MBA* by Josh Kaufman

Learn the basic principles of business without spending six figures on a traditional MBA. Kaufman breaks down business fundamentals in plain English and recommends that you continue studying after this book as a lifelong learner.

7. *Networking Is Not Working* by Derek Coburn

Build meaningful connections by being genuinely interested in others—not by attending awkward events where people merely exchange business cards. Coburn explains that relationships should be based on quality, not quantity.

8. *Money: Master the Game* by Tony Robbins

Robbins encourages readers to find a fiduciary financial advisor and invest in low-cost index funds. He simplifies complex financial strategies and helps you build long-term wealth, even if you're starting from scratch.

9. *Company of One* by **Paul Jarvis**

This is the anti-scale book for business owners who choose to stay small. Jarvis argues that freedom, autonomy, and sustainability are more valuable than just chasing growth and money.

---

10. *The Total Money Makeover* by **Dave Ramsey**

Debt is bad—period. Ramsey explains why you should do everything you can to avoid it. More on his principles in the next section.

I read these books before the advent of AI, ingesting thousands of pages from the world's most popular financial minds.

Some of the advice works, and some of it I question.

The important thing is that I've ingested the knowledge, and I now have the ability to use it in a way that fits my life and my goals.

It's your turn.

What I Learned from Dave Ramsey

I've been watching Dave Ramsey—financial guru and now YouTube personality—take telephone calls since 1993. His philosophy on saving money is simple and hasn't changed in decades: avoid debt.

Ramsey is best known for his *Seven Baby Steps*, a process designed to help anyone achieve financial security and build wealth over time.

Dave Ramsey's Baby Steps to Financial Freedom

Step 1: Save $1,000 in Cash

Dave says everyone should have $1,000 in physical cash on hand, even if it's hidden behind a picture frame. This builds the mindset that you're not broke. The cash also serves as a mini-emergency fund when life happens—like a flat tire, a busted water heater, or an unexpected medical bill.

Step 2: Pay Off All Debt

A devout Christian, Dave often says: *"The borrower is slave to the lender."* You can only build wealth by avoiding debt and its crippling interest. No debt at all—with the only exception being your mortgage. No student loans. No car payments. No credit card balances. According to Dave, if you can't afford to buy something with cash, you shouldn't buy it at all.

Step 3: Build a Fully Funded Emergency Fund

Dave advises building an emergency fund that amounts to 3–6 months of your living expenses—not your salary—in a separate savings account. For example, if your monthly expenses are $3,000, then you should aim to save between $9,000 and $18,000. As the events of 2020 proved, this kind of cushion is essential.

Step 4: Invest 15% of Your Income for Retirement

Dave recommends putting 15% of your gross income into retirement accounts such as a 401(k), 403(b), TSP, or Roth IRA. This is an investment in your future—a payment to your future self—and a way to ensure you won't have to work through your golden years.

Step 5: Save for Your Children's College Fund

Once retirement is in motion, Dave recommends starting a 529 savings plan. This tax-advantaged plan helps you save for your children's college—or any other type of education—

and the funds can be transferred to yourself or nearly any relative if unused. Ramsey's philosophy here is simple: don't go into debt for education—pay in cash by planning early.

Step 6: Pay Off Your Home Early

Dave is a big believer in paying off your mortgage as soon as possible. He says you'll *walk and talk differently* knowing that you have zero debt. Once the house is paid off, you're truly free: No debts, a healthy emergency fund, steady retirement savings, and no more monthly housing payments.

Step 7: Build Wealth and Give Generously

Finally, once you're completely out of debt, have a paid-off house, a fully stocked emergency fund, a college fund, and a retirement fund in place, then—and only then—should you focus on building serious wealth and giving generously to others. This, according to Dave, is the pinnacle of financial peace.

I agree with many of Ramsey's principles. I hate debt, and I do my best to keep a zero balance on my one credit card. But life happens. I've taken on debt for my wedding, for newborn children, and for master's courses—knowing that the extra education would lead to a bump in salary.

I'm not a perfect Dave Ramsey disciple, and I don't expect you to be one either. But it helps to know his principles. They're solid, foundational knowledge for anyone learning how to build wealth from the ground up.

AI as a Career Counselor

If my daughter told me she wanted to study sociology in college, I'd advise her against it.

No disrespect to social workers, but I know it's far more likely you'll find a stable job and earn a livable salary working as an engineer, nurse, or accountant than you would pursuing a career as a social worker, musician or actress.

If you think I'm wrong, do your research—or talk to AI.

Many privileged kids are guided by parents who treat college like an investment. They're told they must study something that leads to a real job and makes enough to support a family.

On the flip side, many underprivileged kids aren't guided at all. They're told that simply graduating college is a success, regardless of the degree earned or the debt incurred. They're encouraged to "follow their passion"—even if that passion leads to nowhere.

The point I'm making is this: If you want sound career advice, talk to AI.

Ask it to pretend to be a career counselor. Ask it what career paths align with your interests, your skills, and your financial goals.

When I was growing up, I had to rely on my parents, a few overworked guidance counselors, and a whole lot of luck to figure out what career would allow me to provide for a family. I read books too.

One of those books taught me that the "perfect job" does three things:

1. It allows you to earn a good salary.

2. It's something you enjoy doing.

3. It's something you're good at.

Think of it as a three-circle Venn diagram. Right in the middle—that's your sweet spot.

Should we all become doctors, lawyers, or engineers? No.

But whatever you choose to do, make sure it checks those three boxes: You like it, you're good at it, and it pays well enough to live decently. Still don't know what path is best for you? Use AI as a career counselor.

Tell it your passions. Ask about salaries and benefits. Have it list pros and cons. Make a choice and go for it. And if things change, adjust. Just don't blame me—or AI—if you make poor choices.

Own your life. Be accountable. And enjoy the process of serving society in exchange for monetary gain.

Thirty years from now, you can ask AI how to enjoy your retirement.

The Perfect Job

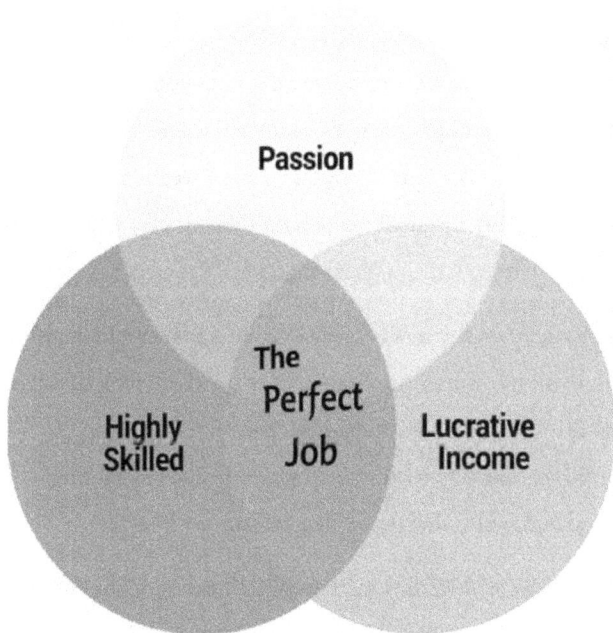

Passion

The
Perfect

Highly   Job   Lucrative
Skilled   Income

AI Alone Won't Make You Rich

AI can give you all the advice you need on how to become rich, but the advice means nothing unless you succeed in your financial goals.

The pursuit of wealth is complex because success means different things to different people.

Some people are content making $80,000 a year with an abundance of free time to pursue their passions and spend with loved ones. Others are not satisfied unless they are making $350,000 a year, working 80-hour weeks and sacrificing years of quality time with their spouse and children to reach that level of financial success.

Then, there are those who are never content—individuals who work not for the money, but for the sheer love of what they do. Think of Warren Buffett, Bill Gates, or Elon Musk—people who continue to push forward even after amassing fortunes beyond imagination.

Clearly, you will need more than AI to become rich—just as you will need more than AI to attract women. AI can be a starting point, a spark, the drop that leads to rain—but it is not a substitute for effort, resilience, and action.

Brilliant Way #4

Use AI as a Psychologist

I've seen psychologists.

You discuss your problems, set some goals, and work toward achieving those goals.

Every week, you talk about your progress, ask questions, and get tools and tips to help you manage your struggles—gratitude journaling, box breathing, reframing negative thoughts, and more.

There are real benefits to seeing a mental health professional—a living, breathing human being—preferably in person, but if needed, online.

I've experienced those benefits myself.

But if you've never experienced the magic of therapy, consider experimenting with talking to AI.

Ask it to pretend to be a psychologist.

Tell it your problems.

Ask it what you should do.

See what it says.

You might walk away with nothing.

Or you might walk away with something that changes everything.

The AI psychologist is available 24/7—and there's no co-pay.

Use AI to Overcome Adversity

I use AI to deal with adversity.

I'll tell AI what happened and ask for another perspective on the issue. Sometimes the response is eye-opening. Sometimes it's ho-hum. But I will say this: with every update to the AI, the responses get better—and more personalized.

We're all limited by our own thoughts. AI can offer new perspectives that might help.

You can even ask AI to motivate you as if it were one of history's greatest speakers. Imagine being coached by a computer-generated version of Martin Luther King Jr., Arnold Schwarzenegger, or Joel Osteen.

Will the impression be perfect? No. But it might offer insight, or at the very least, be interesting or entertaining.

Let's say you asked a girl out and got rejected.

Tell AI what happened. Ask what went wrong. Ask what you could do differently next time.

Maybe the response will be something generic like,
"Her reaction says more about her than it does about you."
Fair. But don't stop there.

Keep prompting AI to help you dig deeper—to extract the lesson from the experience, learn what you can, and come out stronger than you went in.

61

Or suppose you're going through a breakup.

Sure, talk to your friends. That matters.

But after that, try asking AI for its take.

You might be surprised—it could give you better advice than your friends. Or at least a perspective your friends hadn't thought of.

Look, I'm not saying AI is going to fix your heartbreak.

Realistically, I know talking to AI might not do shit.

But it might say something that uplifts you.

And honestly, trying to pick yourself up is almost always better than doing nothing at all.

Let Motion Create Emotion

One mantra of Tony Robbins is: "Let motion dictate your emotion."

In other words—don't wait to feel motivated to act. Act first, and the motivation will follow.

Don't wait to feel like working out. Start moving. By the middle of your workout, you'll feel like you want to keep going.

This philosophy aligns with the classic idea: "Fake it till you make it." Pretending to do something well is often the first step toward doing it well.

For example: Pretend you're a good basketball player. Go play, and get your butt kicked. In the process, you'll learn what a good player looks like, how they move, how they think.

Keep showing up. Keep pretending. Eventually, you won't be faking anymore.

Same goes for attracting women: Pretend to be attractive. Act like someone who knows how to attract women. Look nice. Smell nice. Be nice.

Strike up conversations—even if you're bad at small talk. Learn along the way. Ask questions. Make mistakes.

You'll be surprised by how attractive you actually are—or how attractive women perceive you to be.

Let your motion dictate your emotion.

Don't wait around for your feelings to push you into action. Move first and watch your emotions catch up.

Life is Work

The market is saturated with products that promise quick fixes:

> • Follow this diet, lose weight fast.
> • Take an influencer's advice, gain a million followers.
>
> • Read this book on AI, attract women instantly.

But I'm not here to sell you false hope.

Life is hard work. There are no quick fixes. And if you do find one, it's usually not sustainable.

I've gained weight, lost it, and gained it back again.
I've had money, spent it all, and had to earn it back.
Life—like many things—moves in seasons.

You're happy, then sad, then happy again. Or vice versa.

Life is work. And work is often tiring, unpleasant, and thankless—but necessary.

You can learn to attract women.
You can build confidence, get in shape, make money, and succeed.
But eventually, you'll struggle again. That's just how life works.

The struggle after progress is what author

Seth Godin calls *"the dip."*

There will always be a dip.

The key to sustaining success is **resilience**—being willing to fight through every dip you encounter and keep moving forward.

Bad Things Will Happen

Motivational speaker Les Brown says that *"going through life expecting not to get hurt is like playing football expecting not to get hit."*

You're going to get hurt.

You're going to face adversity.

You're going to experience pain and suffering that goes far beyond a broken heart.

If you live a long and blessed life, you will see both the best and the worst that life has to offer.

People around you will die.

Loved ones will suffer.

You will watch the life get sucked out of vibrant human beings—people you loved more than life itself.

So don't sweat the small stuff.

Rejection and heartbreak are small stuff.

You have to recover from those relatively quickly, because if you're shattered by a breakup, you'll be crushed when real tragedy hits.

Be strong.

Be resilient.

Psychologist Jordan Peterson tells men that the goal is to "be the strongest person at the funeral."

Not because you're unfeeling—but because someone has to be strong enough to carry others.

Adversity can tear people apart. Or it can forge unbreakable bonds.

It can destroy you. Or define you.

Make the most of any bad situation.

Do your best to triumph over trauma.

Be strong for your future woman.

More importantly, be strong for yourself.

How to Be Resilient

Resilience isn't about avoiding hardship; it's about confronting challenges head-on and emerging stronger.

Pound your chest right now. Go ahead. Do it!

Think about what no one can ever take from you.

Your soul.
Your convictions.
Your life mission.

If you don't have a mission—get one. Find something so meaningful that no heartbreak, no failure, no illness, and no tragedy can stop you from pursuing it.

Strip away your money, your family, even your physical body— Who are you then? What part of you is indestructible?

Consider these examples:

- **Malcolm X** entered prison a hustler. He emerged erudite and articulate, with ambition and a mission to change the world. He will be remembered for his unapologetic voice, his intellectual transformation, and his relentless fight for justice.

- **Jay Williams** was considered a future heir to Michael Jordan. Two years into his NBA career, a reckless motorcycle accident ended it. Williams pivoted and became one of the top basketball analysts and commentators in the nation.

- **Nelson Mandela** spent 27 years in prison for fighting South Africa's racist apartheid regime. When he got out, he became the first Black president of South Africa and dismantled apartheid.

- **Stephen Hawking** was diagnosed with ALS at 21 and given just a few years to live. He spent the next 50 years rewriting physics and cosmology—paralyzed, speaking through a cheek muscle, proving that the mind can transcend the body.

There are people who have become paraplegics and quadriplegics—yet still lead full, productive lives. Some say their greatest personal growth happened after their tragedy. Why? Because it forced them to become more than they were.

And what about you?

You're here. Alive. Thinking. Reading.
Show some gratitude for what you have.

Put in the work to fulfill your mission and let nothing get in your way.

Move forward amidst the shit that life will throw at you.

As AI says, "You can lose everything and still come out undefeated—if you refuse to surrender your soul."

AI RIZZ

Brilliant Way #5

Use AI to Learn to Speak to People

Here's the bad news:

Using AI to learn how to talk to people is like using AI to learn how to drive. It can give you tips, but you won't really learn until you get in the driver's seat, start the car, and make mistakes.

The first time you try talking to a pretty girl, you might stammer, "Duh, duh, hello?"
The second time: "Duh, hi."
And maybe by the third, you look her in the eyes, smile, and say confidently, "How's it going?"

Read this chapter. Try a few techniques. Then go live life.

Test things out.

See what works.

See what doesn't work.

We're living in a time when smartphones and social media have zapped people's ability to connect. Basic skills—like making someone laugh or feel special—are becoming rare.

If you master them, you'll stand out.

If you've followed the rest of this book—gotten fit, built wealth, sharpened your mind, and cleaned up your appearance—then knowing how to communicate is gold.

Don't fear connection just because you fear rejection. We're social creatures—we need family, friends, and the kindness of strangers to thrive.

Learn to communicate with everyone—people of every race, class, gender, and creed—not just attractive women.

And if you don't know where to begin?

Ask AI: "How do I learn to talk to people?"

Then go try it in the real world… and learn from your mistakes.

How to Connect with Anyone

Follow this simple small talk technique to connect with anyone:

1. **Compliment**

   Example: "Nice Jordans!" "Interesting bracelet!"
   "Love the new hairstyle." Be careful here. You're
   just trying to acknowledge something positive about
   the other person. **DO NOT** compliment a woman's
   boobs or ass. **DO NOT** compliment another man's
   appearance. Keep it light, genuine, and respectful.

2. **Question**

   Example: "Where'd you get it/them?" "What's with
   the [strange item other person is carrying]?" "Why?"
   This could be an open-ended question or a closed-
   ended one that immediately leads to a more open
   conversation. The goal is to keep the dialogue
   moving, not interrogate.

3. **Listen**

   Don't just hear the response. Look at their eyes, read
   their body language, and pay attention to their tone.
   Are they receptive, rejecting, or neutral? Adjust your
   approach based on what they're giving you.
   Abandon the attempt at conversation if they seem

clearly uninterested, cold, or annoyed.

4. **Respond**

   If the other person is receptive to conversation, keep it going with a statement and/or follow-up question. Imagine you're playing ping pong: **your goal is to keep the ball (the conversation) bouncing back and forth naturally.** Share a little about yourself, ask more about them, and keep it casual.

Now, here's the reality:

Many people either don't want to talk—or don't know how to talk.

If someone clearly doesn't want to engage, give up early. You can take it as a fun challenge to get them to open up, sure—but don't cross the line into looking awkward, inept, intrusive—or worse, harassing. There's a fine line between friendly persistence and making someone uncomfortable.

On the flip side, if you sense someone *wants* to connect but just doesn't know how, you can choose to accept the challenge:

Keep asking questions. Keep making them feel comfortable. Some people enjoy being noticed—and appreciate finding someone they can talk to without fear of judgment.

The technique I just described isn't just for getting a girl's number.

It's for connecting with anyone:

- A family member

- A classmate

- A co-worker

- A neighbor

- A kind stranger

There's nothing wrong with wanting to connect.

As individuals, and as a society, we need connection to survive.

So if you struggle connecting with others, start practicing today—with real people, or even with AI.

The Power of Rapport

Imagine a conversation between a boy and a girl standing next to each other on a college shuttle bus:

Boy: *(sees girl's hoodie that reads "Bayside High School")*
"You went to Bayside?"

Girl: *(cautious, guarded)*
"Yeah." *(Looks away.)*

Boy:

"My best friend Ysely went there." *(He looks for a reaction.)*
"Dominican girl—always smiling."

Girl: *(shrugs)*
"I didn't know her."

Boy:

"She's friends with Karla, this Colombian girl."

Girl: *(silent)*

Boy: *(smiling excitedly)*
"Karla made these homemade buñuelos and sold them on the low to save for college. They were amazing!"

Girl: *(perks up)*
"I loved those buñuelos!"

Boy:

"They're great, aren't they?! If you ever have the craving, I got the hookup."

Girl: *(laughs)*

Boy:

"Are you Colombian too?"

Girl: *(makes eye contact)*
"No, I'm Ecuadorean."

Boy: *(smiling)*
"¡Buenas!"

Girl: *(laughs)*
"Are you Ecuadorean too?"

Boy:

"No, I'm Guatemalan." *(extends hand)*

"I'm Kevin."

Girl: *(shakes his hand)*
"I'm Melanie."

Boy:

"So what's your major?"

(Boy and Girl continue to play conversational ping pong. When the girl departs, the boy smiles and says, "¡Mucho gusto!")

(He doesn't ask for her Instagram or phone number—yet. What matters is he built genuine rapport, made a real connection, and practiced making life a little more enjoyable—for himself and for the people around him.)

Notice how the boy assessed the girl before talking to her. Directly asking a stranger, "What school did you go to?" is intrusive—but because her hoodie made it obvious, the question felt natural.

It was even more justified when the boy mentioned that his "best friend" went to the same school named on the girl's hoodie.

The girl didn't know the boy's friends by name, but he kept looking for common ground—and eventually, he found it:

- They both know Bayside High School.

- They both know about the homemade buñuelos sold at the school.

- They both love Karla's homemade buñuelos.

- They both come from a similar Latin American background.

And now—because of the boy's connections—the girl knows he has access to something she enjoys.

If she ever really wants those buñuelos again, she now has a reason to continue the connection.

That's rapport: finding commonalities, even small ones, that naturally make people feel connected.

You've probably met someone who either successfully built rapport with you—or crashed and burned trying.

When two people meet and start dropping names, places, or experiences, they're searching for something in common. Find that shared thing, and the bond instantly becomes stronger.

It's a subconscious thought:

"I like this person because they know X, and I know X too."

That "X" could be:

- A person

- A place

- A hobby

- A food

- A sport

- Anything you point to as a shared experience

And rapport isn't just for dating.

It's a powerful tool for:

- Strengthening family ties

- Deepening friendships

- Building professional connections

Will you have a 100% success rate in building rapport?

Of course not!

Sometimes you'll search for common ground and realize you don't have much in common.

Other times, you'll make real connections—and every once in a while, one of those connections may just be a beautiful woman who's happy you started the conversation and is willing to hang out with you to talk more.

The Perfect Place to Take Her

Question: Where is the perfect place to take a date?
Answer: It depends.

No two women are alike. Some prefer a lively concert. Others prefer a quiet café. Some love museums.
Always have three to four possible date venues in mind before you meet up.

You don't want to be that guy with only one or two ideas—then find out she's not impressed with either.
And you definitely don't want the scenario where you ask, *"Where would you like to go?"* she says, *"Wherever,"* — and you draw a blank and blame her for her indecision.

Many women are naturally indecisive.
How could they not be? They've been told what to do, how to act, what hairstyle to wear, and how to dress since birth.

So be a man and take charge.
Take her to the place she wants to go—even if she doesn't know she wants to go there yet.
And how would you know?
You assess her psychological profile first.

Audio, Visual, Kinesthetic Profiles

According to *How to Make People Like You in 90 Seconds or Less* by Nicholas Boothman, there are three main types of people: **Auditory, Visual, and Kinesthetic.**

- About **20%** of the population are **Auditory**.
  They're most turned on by what they hear.
  They love music, probably aren't the best dressers, and usually walk around with an AirPod in one ear.
  When seeking agreement, they say things like, *"You hear me?"* or *"Are you listening?"*

  If you're dating an auditory woman, take her somewhere with great music—live bands, lounges, cool playlists. She'll like you without even realizing why.

- About **70%** of people are **Visual**.
  They're stimulated by what they see.
  They're usually good dressers, color-coordinated, and notice when a hair is out of place.
  When seeking understanding, they say things like, *"I see what you mean."*

  Take visual women to beautiful places—restaurants with stunning décor, botanical gardens, museums, art galleries, sculpture parks.

- The remaining **10%** are **Kinesthetic**.

  They're focused on how things feel, not necessarily how they look or sound. They might wear hoodies, soft fabrics, and comfy clothes. When they connect, they say things like, *"Do you feel me?"*

  They love cozy places: cafes with plush chairs, low lighting, places where the ambiance feels comforting.

It's worth noting: nobody is 100% auditory, visual, or kinesthetic. People are blends—maybe 50% auditory, 40% visual, 10% kinesthetic, and so on.

Someone might prefer a concert one night... and a cozy, quiet spot the next. Another person might be so kinesthetic-heavy that they struggled in traditional school settings because education mainly favors auditory (lectures) and visual (reading) learning.

Think about the girl you want to ask out.

- Does her outfit always match?

- Always has music playing?

- Wears comfy, casual clothes?

Talk to her. Build rapport. Mirror her world.

- If she's auditory, say: *"I hear you."*

- If she's visual, say: *"I see your point."*

- If she's kinesthetic, say: *"I feel you."*

Subconsciously, she'll feel more connected to you—and she won't even know why.

If she says no?

Shrug, smile, move on.

If she says yes?

Take her somewhere that stimulates her psychological profile.

Use Yelp for Restaurant Reviews

Use Yelp or Google Reviews to find the best places based on music, decor, and comfort.

I've tried using AI to find good restaurants—it's getting there, but honestly, Yelp and Google are still better for local, up-to-date info.

I trust Yelp's filtering system—it's good at flagging fake reviews and boosting authentic ones.

Look for reviews by "Yelpers" — not shady five-star reviews left by the owner's cousin.

Research before you entertain a woman.

Differentiate yourself from the pack of guys who only know Applebee's or Cheesecake Factory.

Imagine the difference:

Instead of basic chains, you're taking her to snack on Pandebono from a Colombian café, sticky mango rice from a Thai restaurant, or a dessert made with ube from a Filipino bakery.

Take her to mansions, gardens, museums, observatories, art galleries, and sculpture parks.

Take her somewhere new—somewhere that makes her think:

This man is different.

87

There's No Substitute for Real People

No one does it alone.

If you think you're "self-made," you're not seeing the full truth: somewhere, somehow, someone helped you along the way.

There are forces in this universe—both for you and against you—that you may not even be aware of.

Life happens outside of your own little bubble.

Be a good person.

Do as much good as you can for as many people as you can.

You'll raise the chances that good will be done back onto you.

AI is an incredible tool.

But it will never be a substitute for real people.

Neither will social media, online learning, or OnlyFans.

Nothing.

You must learn to interact with real people.

And you can only learn if you're willing to make mistakes.

So go out and interact.

Learn what to do—and what not to do—

from real human beings.

Study what works and what doesn't

in conversation, in connection, in life.

You will make mistakes.

But that's the price of learning—and the path to getting

better at dealing with people.

Not just women, but your family.

Your friends.

Your coworkers.

Your boss.

Your kids.

Use AI to understand people.

But master the art of dealing with them

—live and in the flesh.

Recovering from Rejection

I know what it's like to be rejected.

I wrote an entire book—*How to Attract Women If You're Not That Attractive*—based on personal experience.

And I was getting rejected in an era *before* AI,

So I'm not going to tell you that ChatGPT will soften the blow.

Because the truth is: rejection is part of life.

You will get rejected.

Women you want will say no.

Your first few girlfriends might dump you.

And if they don't, *you* might end up dumping them.

Because rejection goes both ways. And staying in a relationship just to avoid hurting someone? That's not noble. That's cowardly.

Even the girl of your dreams has the right to say: "I don't want to be with you."

And you, by the same token, have that right too.

Not every woman you want will want you back.
And that's okay.
Because one day, you'll meet someone who does.
And you'll *want* her too.
That's what makes it meaningful.

So don't crumble. Don't spiral. Don't let one rejection become your identity.

Feel the pain.
Accept it.
Let it fuel you to become better.
Wiser. Stronger.
More resilient.
Then—move on.

The sting fades.
The lesson stays.
And the right person—eventually—will see your value.

And when that happens?
You'll be glad the others said no.

Prepare for Rejection

Chances are, you've already been rejected.
And that's OK.
You're still here, reading this book—and growing from it.

Prepare to keep getting rejected.
That's life.

In *The Sport of Business*, billionaire Mark Cuban said he loves entrepreneurship because **you only need to win once**.
You could start 100 companies and fail—but if one of them hits, you win. That's all that matters.

Dating is the same.
If your goal is to find *one* great woman to spend your life with, it doesn't matter how many women reject you.
You just need one win.

So every "no" gets you closer to the one "yes" that changes everything.

In baseball, a .300 hitter is elite—that's three hits in ten tries.
In basketball, a 50% shooter is dependable.
In love?
You only need to hit once.

So swing.
Miss.
Swing again.
Miss again.

And when you finally connect—
It's a walk-off home run.

If She Cheats on You

Let's say you got her number, took her out, started dating, and everything seemed solid—until you found out she cheated.

What now?

Move on.
Don't try to win her back.
Don't try to fight the other guy—as if that'll accomplish anything.

If you're a man of character—fit, intelligent, financially stable, emotionally disciplined—you deserve better.

And if your first response is, *"I don't want better. I want her,"* my response is simple:
You don't have a choice.

She made her choice when she betrayed your trust.
Your only power now is to make a better one:

Leave. Learn. Grow.

Attract someone who respects you.
Talk to a therapist if needed.
Vent to AI.

Channel the pain into something productive:

- Work out more.

- Play ball.

- Work overtime.

- Start business.

- Take that trip.

- Chill with your boys.

There are entire books about moving on.
The Breakup Repair Kit: How to Heal a Broken Heart
by Marni Kamis is one of them.
Synopsis: Rebuild. Reclaim. Reinvent.

Sure, you *could* try to "work it out." But let me ask you:

- Are you married?

- Do you have kids?

- A mortgage? Shared bank accounts?

If the answer's no—and you're young, single, and busting your ass to be your best—why stay with a woman who already showed you who she is?

If she cheats on you as a girlfriend,

and you give her a pass,

she'll cheat on you as a wife—

and ruin your ass.

So don't seek revenge.

Don't beg for closure.

Just exit.

Work on yourself.

And step into a world

full of better options.

Don't Navigate the Friendzone

Men and women can't *really* be "just friends."

When we're kids, sure—you can play in the sandbox together.
But as we get older, the dynamic changes.
One person eventually catches feelings.
And if the other person doesn't feel the same—
someone gets hurt, and the friendship fades.

Ask yourself this:
If you're in a serious relationship, would you want your
partner spending hours alone with someone of the opposite
sex "just for the company"?

Probably not.

Ask your girl the same question.
Her answer's likely the same.

That's why you shouldn't navigate the friendzone.
Don't hang around hoping to "earn" your way into a
relationship. It doesn't work like that.

If you're interested in a woman romantically—be clear.

Ask her for her number. Invite her out.

If she says no? Respect it.
But don't linger under the illusion of friendship
while secretly hoping for more.

Could a platonic connection *eventually* turn romantic? Sure. But that's rare—and usually only happens when two single people grow closer organically over time.

Don't bet on it.

Instead, take this approach:

- If she's single and the vibe is good, shoot your shot.

- If she declines, fall back.

- If she shows renewed interest weeks later, try again.

- But after three strikes? You're out.

Never harass.

Never beg.

Never chase.

You're not trying to be her "friend."

You're trying to be the man she talks to *her* friends about.

Real World Rizz

Don't sit behind a screen all day trying to pick up girls.

There's a name for guys like that—and it's not a compliment.

If you want to attract women, you're going to have to get in the trenches.

That means waking up, getting dressed, and going *outside*.

Working from home? That's a disadvantage.

You've got to get out into the world and interact.

You'll have to start conversations.

You'll have to risk rejection.

You'll have to toe the line between confident and creepy.

And yes—you might look like a fool. Or a tool.

But that's the price of entry.

You'll have to develop thick skin.

You may get cynical.

You'll realize a lot of men today don't know how to talk to women.

And for a while—you might be one of them.

But don't quit.

Be resilient.

Learn from every failed interaction.

Every wrong step can still move you forward—if you learn from it.

Edison famously said:

"I didn't fail 10,000 times. I found 9,999 ways that didn't work."

You are going to be Edison.

You are going to go out there and fail.

And then one day—

you're going to go out there and succeed.

Shoot Your Shot

I tell young men:
Don't be the guy who crushes on a girl for three years in high school—only to finally ask her to prom, get rejected, and realize he wasted four years chasing a dream that was never real.

You'd rather be the *jerk* who regularly asks girls out—gets rejected sometimes, but also gets dates, stories, and confidence along the way. He *lives*.

There's a reason these jerks get girls:
They take a lot of shots.
And those who shoot often... eventually hit.

These guys aren't necessarily more attractive than you.
They just put themselves out there more often.

And women—many of whom are craving attention, fishing for compliments, or just hoping to meet a decent guy—often go with them because no better option shows up.

So be the good guy who shoots his shot.
If you're fit, intelligent, and employed, you have a lot to offer.
Live a life you're proud of—and then advertise it.

Because no one can buy what you're selling if they don't know it's for sale.

Shoot your shot.
And if you're not good yet—keep shooting.

Eventually, you'll hit a game-winner.

How to Ask for a Woman's Number

I know this book is about using AI to get better with women—but AI isn't going to be the one asking for her number.

At some point, you'll need to rely on human skill—your own. That means knowing how to start a conversation, keep it flowing, and ask her out.

If you're going to approach a woman—whether she's a stranger or someone familiar—you'll probably have to make the first move. That means eye contact, a "hello," and then either:

- Compliment (bold move) or
- Question (safer—you can justify the interaction with curiosity).

From there, build rapport.
Find something to connect on—the shitty weather, a mean boss, a shared frustration.
Look for clues: a bracelet repping her culture, a pin for her favorite artist, a college or city name on her hoodie.
Ask a question—not to get her number, but because you're a decent human being who knows how to start a conversation.

People barely talk anymore.
Genuine conversation makes an impression.

Learn to read body language and tone. If she's smiling, laughing, holding eye contact—you're good. If she's ignoring you, being curt, or glued to her phone—cut your losses. No one wants to be on a viral clip titled *"Creep on Public Transportation #SMFH."*

Now, talking to someone you'll never see again is different from talking to someone you'll see often—classmate, coworker, neighbor.

If you're not likely to see her again and the vibe is strong, shoot your shot. Try something honest:

"I don't usually take this bus, so I might never see you again. Would it be crazy if I asked to stay in touch?"

Women aren't stupid. They know when someone's into them. But if you've got your life together, many will be flattered—and open to more.

If it's someone you *do* see regularly, play the long game. If approaching a stranger is a half-court heave, winning over someone familiar is a seven-game series. Build slowly. Read her energy. Don't force anything. Don't shit where you eat.

If you do get the number, **call her in three days**.

Not one or two—too eager.

Not seven—you look distracted or disinterested.

Three days says, "I've got a life, but I'm thinking about you."

And yes, I said call. Not DM.

In-person > phone call > text > DM.

FaceTime? Only if you need to confirm she's not a catfish.

How to Ask a Woman Out

So you got a woman's phone number—Congratulations! But you're not done yet. A number isn't a promise; it's a possibility.

She could ignore your call.
She could say she's not "interested like that."
She could've given you a fake number.
Or worse—her boyfriend's number.
(If you know, you know.)

But if she does pick up and actually enjoys talking to you, good! Keep her engaged. Ask about her day. Ask what she's been up to. Ask about her weekend plans.

"What are you doing this weekend?"

Timing matters. Ask her on a Tuesday or Wednesday. Most people make weekend plans by Thursday.

If she lists off plans for all three days—cool. Move on. Maybe try again in a few weeks. If she picks up and still dodges plans—cut your losses.

And if she never picks up or doesn't call you back?
Delete her number and move on.

They say "winners never quit"—but winners quit all the time. They just quit early on things that don't matter so they can go hard on what does. That includes women. If she doesn't see your value, don't waste time.

Another solid line—if you're with her in person:

"Where you headed now?"

If she says "going home to do nothing," that's your shot to invite her out. Casual. No pressure.
Grab a bite. A coffee. A beer. A moment.

And if you drive and she doesn't?

"Need a ride?"

That says a lot—especially if it's your car, your insurance, and your independence. Being able to provide for yourself and others is rare these days. Add in good hygiene, consistent exercise, emotional intelligence, and the ability to hold a real conversation—and you stand out.

And if she still says no to all of that?

Move on. It's her loss.

If you're on a path to becoming a stronger, better man, keep your head up.

Not every woman will be into you.
And you won't want to date *every* woman either.

Life is fair because it's unfair to everybody.

Shoot your shot.
Make or miss,
Keep playing.

You only have to win once.

AI RIZZ

Final Word

Obviously,
AI alone won't help you attract women.

But it's a starting point.

Using AI could begin
a learning process that changes your life.

Most of us aren't born with charisma.
Most of us aren't taught it either.
But all of us can develop rizz—
if we work hard enough.

Use AI to learn quickly.
Read books for deeper learning.
See what works—and what doesn't.
Don't get discouraged by mistakes—
they're a natural part of success.

Work out. Eat right.
Work hard. Make money.
Get your mind right.
Learn to talk to people.
Learn from experience.

Make yourself valuable in today's dating market.

Given the state of many young men today—
it's not that hard to do.

And being that you've finished this book,
Surely, one day, a beautiful woman will fall for you.

Acknowledgements*

To the love of my life, *Sharon*—
thank you for giving me the happiest years of my life.

To my son, *John*—
may you continue to be a dream come true.

To my daughters, *Isabella* and *Victoria*—
please, marry right.

To my brothers, *Jerome* and *Juan*—
God could not have given me two better wingmen.

To my parents, *Juan* and *Lucia*—
God could not have blessed me with better parents.

To my godparents, *Tito Lito* and *Tita Vicky*—
thank you for being my parents in the Philippines.

To my third set of parents, Tita *Loida* and *Tito Bing*—
I am grateful beyond words for your love and care.

To my cousins, *Chris, Pat, Norman, Con, Ringo, and JR*—
through the good, the bad, and the ugly.

To my ride-or-die, *Brian Greenspan*—
for your early lessons on AI.

To my *Ninong, Brian Shea*—
for being an eternal blessing in my life.

To *Raphael Villa*—
for introducing me to ChatGPT.

To *CUNY Queens College*—
for granting me three degrees, nine years of an elite
education, and a lifetime of value by teaching me *how to fish*.

To *SUNY Old Westbury*—
thank you to the entire English Department for your support.

I'm especially grateful to:

> • *Professor Jessica Williams*, for holding her students to
> high standards.

> • *Professor Elizabeth Schmermund*, for the life lessons
> that was Greek mythology class.

> • *Professor Erin Fiero*, for her pedagogical excellence.

- *Professor Darshna Katwala*, for her compassion and curriculum that made learning feel like a conversation.

- *Professor Jacqueline Emery*, Chair of the English Department, for running a program rooted in academic integrity and support.

Mary and *Brad* at the Writing Center—
for your time, encouragement, and wisdom.

Scott Bickards, Recreation Coordinator—
your hiking trips cleared my mind, restored my energy, and allowed me to appreciate the beautiful scenery of Long Island.

And finally, to *Sam Altman*—
for altering the world. In my eyes, so far, for the better.

About the Author

Enrique Voltaire spent years failing in dating until he read dating books and discovered the *secrets* to attracting women. After living his dream as an international playboy, he retired from the game and married the most beautiful woman in the world.

Voltaire writes with humor and honesty about modern masculinity, self-improvement, and tools that can give even a short Asian guy an edge.

He is the author of *How to Attract Women If You're Not That Attractive* and *AI Rizz: Five Brilliant Ways to Use AI to Attract Women.*

When he's not writing, he enjoys walking with his potcake Boaz, reading the *Wall Street Journal*, and watching WWE, NXT, and even AEW.

For inquiries, speaking engagements, or consultations, email him at *EnriqueVoltaireAuthor@gmail.com.*

www.ingramcontent.com/pod-product-compliance
Lightning Source LLC
Chambersburg PA
CBHW030837300326
41935CB00037B/572